BE THE MAN

BE THE MAN

STOP *LYING,*
START *LEADING*
TODAY

BY GARRETT J WHITE

FOUNDER OF WAKE UP WARRIOR

Be The Man
Stop Lying, Start Leading Today

Copyright ©2019 by Garrett J White
Wake Up Warrior™
www.wakeupwarrior.com

Published by Brand Elevate, Publishing Division
Irvine, CA
www.BrandElevate.com

ISBN: 978-1-68102-956-6

Printed in the United States of America

WWW.WARRIORBOOK.COM

TABLE OF CONTENTS

BE THE MAN

FOREWORD

BY SAM FALSAFI

I Was A Liar And About To Be Exposed.

My Brother,

It was January 2015, as we were preparing for WARRIOR WEEK 16, this crucible event we run every single month to create the PATH to beyond the POSSIBILITY of LIBERATION for MEN, the lights went OFF. Our Training room was in the DARK.

The Lights Were Off!

We had no electricity, so I called SDG&E and found out that we had not paid our $75 electricity bill...and yet here we were, preparing for a half-million dollar event... my first reaction was:

1

"BRO!!! What The Hell Man?!"

Forgetting a small detail began compromising the entire experience, not only for me but for all of the men in attendance. Accessing the mailbox in the old Warrior HQ was a pain in the ass, so none of our team made the effort to check up on the contents inside of it for months… which is where the reminders for the electric bill were.

We couldn't run our event without power, so I told Garrett, "I got this."

I Had Difficulty Breathing

I called up the customer service agent, knowing that simply telling her that we didn't check our mail wouldn't be reason enough to send an immediate response to the HW, so I proceeded to tell her the most horrific, fabricated bullshit:

"We need the electricity up NOW!

We operate a daycare for babies that have difficulty breathing and we need our dehumidifiers to FUNCTION at all times. We need power."

I went on about these poor babies until we got the 45-minute service versus the 2-3 day normal business day maintenance.

As I hung up, proud of what I accomplished, I thought to myself,

"YEAH Man…I SAVED This Event!"

When I told Garrett the power will soon be back on, he turned and looked at me, quietly saying: "You know that was a fucking lie. You lied to this person and for her, this is the version of the truth within you that she knows. She will run with this in the universe, and that lie will remain wandering in the universe regarding this event forever."

My Lies Were Like A Stack Of Bricks

That fucking hit me like a brick …I was already living the WARRIOR'S WAY for 9 months, as a graduate of WARRIOR WEEK 5.

My life had completely changed, leaving a decade as a reputable business man in the Oil & Gas industry after deciding to help Garrett grow the WARRIOR MOVEMENT.

I felt a calling towards serving others that I had never seen in me after my WarriorWeek experience, finding the COURAGE to let go of the security that I knew most in my life by becoming a trainer within Wake Up Warrior™.

Without even realizing it, I had chosen to follow the operating system that I had adopted from society: that in order to be successful, I must make more money… at the cost of everything, including integrity. This lie had remained within me.

I didn't see it until that day.

The Definition of Courage

Courage has many names, defined in many ways.

Courage implies facing a risk. Courage is measured against danger, which is what I found at my Warrior Week, seeing how necessary it is to go through HELL to find it. As I went there to the very Gates of Hell within me, I declared that

"I Am Here To Fill Up My Bucket With FIRE…

…I am here to claim WHO I AM…I am the Beginning, I am the END, I am the hidden, I am the revealed, I AM THAT I AM."

I felt that declaration, learning directly from Garrett J White as my teacher for the next 9 months that in order to have courage, I must STOP FUCKING LYING. And what did I do that morning the power shut off? I replaced courage with cowardice because a lie was more important to me than my own personal character.

I let Garrett down by lying. I had broken the CODE: this decree that we live by here at WARRIOR that says, "Stop fucking lying. Tell the TRUTH."

I FUCKED UP.

I knew better. And yet when I was faced with adversity, I told a lie to make an event that was built on discovering the truth inside occur.

4

It was such a profound experience for me that I made a promise to GOD and MYSELF that I will never LIE again about anything, small or BIG …I will always tell the TRUTH.

Tattooing Honesty On My Arm

As a symbol of HONESTY and INTEGRITY, at the age of 38 I got my first tattoo: a LION placed on my forearm, so obvious and BIG that I could never hide it, just like the TRUTH.

There are thorns on the path of the truth—not few, but many—but therein the tests of love and truth are found. Those wishing to find the flowers of the TRUTH will have to pass through these thorns, and it's going to be painful. It will last a while. No one will be there to save you from yourself. Truth is not cheap. It never was, and it never will be. We must PAY the price—and stop being afraid.

Beyond The Crucifixion Is The King's Throne.

My Brother, My Mentor, My Teacher,My Friend, My Family…

Garrett's presence in my life has completely changed who I AM and how I show up for my family. After all of these years of being by his side and through every evolution of the Warrior Movement, I have witnessed Garrett's commitment to LEAD this movement of MODERN MEN in searching for the HAVE IT ALL lifestyle.

He has truly opened my eyes and guided me to LEAD my FAMILY to places I would have never gone without the CODE…

He fights relentlessly for a MAN to love his wife and family, to appreciate this GIFT from GOD to nourish and GROW as a HUSBAND, as a FATHER, as a PRODUCER.

Defining Manhood

What does it mean to BE THE MAN for me?

It means to follow a path of integrity: a blueprint to modern masculinity by having the courage to always tell the truth. Established men of wealth and power, ideological men of religion are a few examples of influences a modern man is exposed to, yet amidst all of this, there is also a list of obedience, duty,moral endeavors, self-denial and self-sacrifices that will be imposed by these influences.

What if being a man was a JOURNEY…A WAY…A PATH to be paved every single day with a daily dialogue with THE VOICE within?

Finding The Voice Of God

There's a Voice inside of us, guiding us towards expansion and becoming the better version of ourselves. Many call this Voice GOD. You see, it's one thing to know *information* about GOD and it's also one thing to *practice* different spiritual rituals or uphold certain religious traditions, but sadly, many that have "found" religion still remain empty. It is almost like religion gives men information about GOD — but it does not give them the ability to personally **encounter** GOD by listening to the VOICE within.

- WHAT IF You GIVE Yourself PERMISSION to SEEK?
- WHAT IF the GOD you may have known through religion from a formidable distance can be encountered personally through THE VOICE you will hear within you?
- WHAT IF BEING a MAN was simply the WAY of the VOICE?
- WHAT IF...

Council of Kings, Not Slaves

If this message in these first few pages resonates with you in your HEART and pulls you towards a discovery journey where your thoughts are no longer the destination, simply because thoughts will never take you beyond the known into the forgotten unknown...

WELCOME HOME.

Welcome to the CONVERSATION OF MEN not SLAVES.

A MAN who is more concerned with being a GOOD MAN than being GOOD at being a MAN makes a very well-behaved SLAVE.

My Brother, as you open this book, welcome to the COUNCIL of KINGS.

Welcome to a place where the TRUTH becomes part of your past as you tell it and if YOU lie, just like I did on that day with customer service to get the power on, then the LIE becomes part of your FUTURE.

Path To The Future

The Path of Heaven inevitably passes through hell. Those who are skilled at closing their eyes find themselves in hell and get stuck there.

OPEN YOUR EYES, My Brother.

When you can walk into a room and you have nothing to hide, you ARE the most powerful person in the room.

WELCOME to the Brotherhood of TRUTH.

Coach Sam "The Terrorist" Falsafi

SHEEPDOG, SHEPHERD and LEAD TRAINER[1] of Wake Up Warrior

---

1   Go to http://warriorweeknow.comto listen to the weekly Parable from the Pit podcast with Coach Sam and Warrior Guests. You can also go to https://warriorweek.comto fill out an application for Warrior Week.

INTRODUCTION

BY GARRETT J WHITE

A Difficult Yet Transformational Truth You Won't Hear At Church Or In Your Mastermind Group:

My Brother,

It's time to fucking get started.

I'm not sure what led you to this book or who may have given it to you.

In reality?

It doesn't matter. What does matter?

That you're here and you're reading these words now.

So let's stop screwing around and get after it.

I'm going to start our time together with a question…

Do You Know The Real Reason Marriages Fail, Businesses Collapse And Men Continue To "Play Small?"

Take A Guess…

Based on the title of this book, the obvious answer would be, "Because Men Lie"…

…But that would only be partially correct. Lying is just part of the equation.

It leads to a much heavier and hidden Condition that causes men to lead lives of addiction, sedation, destruction and mediocrity…

And like many health conditions, once you find out you have it, you're going to do one of two things.

1. Take Action And Do Whatever It Takes To Defeat It.

2. Bury Your Head In The Sand And Act Like It's Not There…Until It Kills You.

What Is This Condition I Speak Of?

…I'll tell you in just a minute. Plus, I'll share why small business owners and men who have "good" lives are at the most risk.

First, I want to let you know WHY I wrote this book and what you can expect to get out of it.

The Common Thread

One of the many benefits of being in the trenches with droves of men who are fighting to transform their lives is the real life evidence I have gathered and examined to find trends that allow me to build solutions and teach more effectively.

I've literally worked with thousands of men who have gone from…

- Obese to fit. Broke to rich. Depressed and suicidal to living with a purpose. Addicted to sober.

- Unfaithful in their marriage to faithful

- Playing it safe living a "Good" life to going all in and living a GREAT life.

I even have my own stories of divorce, an estranged son, infidelity and losing every penny of a multi-million dollar empire before rebuilding myself, my marriage and starting the Wake Up Warrior™ Movement.

(More On My Story In Section 1)

Regardless of the results these men and I achieved, and the path we took to get them…

There are two things we all had in common...

…Two threads that tied us all together.

[1] We Feel Alone In Our Pain

It felt as if nobody else was experiencing our thoughts… our pain…our fear…our boredom …and our uncertainty.

As a result, we LIED. We constantly LIED To ourselves…

To others…

Anything to avoid being vulnerable and looking like we didn't have our shit together.

- We plastered fake smiles on our faces.

- We posted our highlight reels on social media.

- We lied about how well we're doing.

- We acted like we cared about shit we really didn't give a fuck about.

- We made commitments that deep down we wanted no part of.

- We popped pills to wake up and drank or smoked to go to bed.

Our feelings…our opinions…our energy…our desires… our "strategies"…ALL FAKE and built on lies to pretend we didn't feel alone. Look,

There's many reasons a man lies like this, all of which we'll cover throughout this book.

The Primary Reason We Lied? (and most men lie)

Because we felt alone and like nobody would understand or accept us if they knew how we really felt and what we really wanted.

So, we sunk into isolation…

…putting on a show and burying the truth in hopes nobody ever found out.

Brother,

I want you to consider this,

You Don't Have To Be Hiding In The Back Of Your Closet To Feel Alone And Isolated. There can be family, friends, co-workers and employees all around you, all the time and yet you can still feel completely alone.

How?

Because, underneath the lies you live and tell to "fit in"…under the sedation and numbing of the feelings and emotions you don't give yourself permission to experience and express…**is the man you want to be**.

That man is your authentic self who you've suppressed… and he's the one who feels isolated and alone from being buried deep inside of you under a complex web of lies and stories.

Entrepreneurs Are At The Most Risk...

In many ways,

Small business owners and entrepreneurs are at the most risk of sedation, suppression and feeling alone.

Here's why.

As an entrepreneur **you experience pressure and expectations** coming from multiple angles.

Whether it's at home or in your business — you're supposed to be "the man" who has all the answers.

You're Supposed To Have Your Shit Together And In Total Control.

There's **no room for your emotions and feelings** of doubt, fear, anger, excitement, uncertainty and frustration...especially as an entrepreneur.

So you put a mask on and sedate, suppress and act like you got it all figured out to please everyone else's expectations of you.

Entrepreneurs also have the added element of "acceptable sedation" playing against them.

Most Of These Entrepreneur's Sedate With Work And "The Grind."

They bury themselves in productivity and the pursuit of making money.

And they get praised for it.

They have permission from society that not only is it acceptable, it's honorable.

Which makes it more difficult to even recognize that it's damaging behavior, let alone break-free from it.

But under the lie of "just trying to provide a good life for my family" is the fact you're just avoiding the feeling of disconnection at home.

You're avoiding dealing with shit in your marriage, your health and your kids.

Lastly,

A Lot Of Entrepreneurs Have The Appearance Of Being "GOOD."

They normally make good money.

Married, kids, the cars and the house.

Which creates an atmosphere that doesn't give them any space to be in pain or the desire to expand and create MORE without judgement, shame and guilt from others.

The judgement can also come from themselves too.

Like,

- "How dare you want more — why can't you just be happy with what you have?!"

- "What's wrong with you?! — Most people would DIE to have your problems…"

As if the amount of money we make or the businesses we own means we can't have desires, fear and pain.

Again,

This dynamic only reinforces the feeling that we're alone, something is wrong with us and nobody can understand.

Which only drives us deeper into our pit of isolation and sedation.

Here's Why This "Alone" Conversation Matters...

The power you seek to produce the results you want can only be found in your authentic self.

See,

There Is A Man Inside You Right Now Who Is 10x The Producer You Are.

- He's a better father.

- He's a better husband.

- He's a better businessman.

- He has better sex.

- He's a better athlete and in better shape.

That man is already inside of you. He just needs to be ACTIVATED.

No Part Of Your Life Can Be Transformed Until You Extract The Power From Your True Authentic Self

This Is Why The WarriorBook Is Such A Powerful Tool.

Not only does it give you tools and systems to activate the 10x producer inside of you…

…It also gives men the opportunity once they acquire the Full Teaching in the Warrior Book to experience what it feels like to be part of a brotherhood. To join a group of men who are on the same journey as them and readily available for support.

Ok.

A couple of pages ago I told you there were two things that we as men all have in common.

I shared the first with you and now let's jump into the second.

[2] We Lie & Hide The Truth Inside

See,

Every man's path is going to be different.

However, the gateway at which they stand, waiting to get access to their path to power is ALWAYS the same.

It's called **TELLING THE FUCKING TRUTH.**

Brother,

Before You Can Even Think About Making Any Meaningful Changes In Your Life, You Must Have The Courage To Tell TRUTH to unlock the gate to your path.

But most motivational speakers don't want to go to that Gate.

Most books, seminars and courses skip over that part.

Your Church Wants Nothing To Do With The Gate.

Can those "things" make you feel good?

-Yes.

Can they give you "ah-ha moments"

-Yes.

Can they light a fire under your ass?

-Yes.

Can all those "things" point you in the right direction?

-Yes.

But I'll have you consider this…

…Directions Are No Good If You Can't Tell The Fucking Truth About Where You're At!

As powerful as Google Maps is to have the ability to give you the exact directions down to the square-foot to anywhere you want to go in the world… it's virtually powerless if you can't punch in where you're starting from.

Makes sense, right?

Simple enough concept, right?

Just Tell The Truth, No Need For A Book On This, Right?

Not exactly… Here's Why.

Most of the lies we tell and believe to be true are **covert**, meaning it's not like we're consciously making lies up about where we ate last night.

It's much more complex than that. We lie about…

- What we truly want

- Who we are.

- What we're truly capable of.

- How we truly feel.

- Where we want to go.

- What we're afraid of.

And more…

Most men started telling these lies and burying their truth's as boys just to avoid being judged and to please their parents, teachers, church, friends and coaches.

(I dive into this much deeper a little later in the book)

Your Lies Shape Your BELIEF SYSTEM.

To the extent that the truth has been buried so deep and for so long that it's completely unrecognizable.

And here's where the shit really starts to get dangerous…

…This is the answer to the question why marriages fail, businesses collapse and men continue to play small.

Which means…

- What we believe is possible

- What we believe is weak

- What we believe is strong

- What we believe is real or fake

- What we believe is love

- What we believe is hard work

- What we believe is commitment

- What we believe we deserve

All Of It Is Dictated By Your Belief System...

which in turn dictates what you think and what you DO.

Why else are we more overweight and unhealthy than we've ever been despite having more information and programs readily available to us?

Because, unless our belief systems change — we can't.

Why else do you think so many men are sedating with porn, substance abuse, social media, work, food and video games?

Because they've suppressed their truth, leading lives based on lies that are too painful and uncomfortable to

21

deal with — so they try to get lost in shit that suspends them from their reality.

Why else can a marriage look like it failed overnight?... (when really it was years and decades in the making)

Because, most men ignore the red-flags and bury them under lies like they've done with everything else that threatened their belief system.

Why else can a Man want something so bad...more sex, more money, better marriage, better body, better spiritual connection, etc. But can't seem to take the action necessary to obtain it...even when they know what to do?

Because, when your desires don't completely align with your belief systems — it doesn't matter how bad you want something — you can't get it until you expand your beliefs.

Let's Look At A Quick Example Involving Beliefs About Money.

Imagine the man who grew up without money.

All the people in his family, church and community would talk shit about"evil rich people."

...how "they're the problem with the world today."

All of which planted a seed of belief that money is evil.

After years of exposure and nourishment, that seed grew into a full-blown belief buried deep in his consciousness and psychology.

I See This All The Time In Small Business Owners.

One day they start a business and claim "they're not in it for the money."

"They just want to help people."

Their deep seeded belief won't let them be in it for money or even want to make a lot of it.

So they under value their service. Undercharge.

Never raise their rates.

Never invest in marketing.

And then one day they have a family and realize they need to make more money.

But there's still an underlying belief that money is evil and subconsciously he doesn't want to turn into the guys he and his family used to hate.

Do You See How This Can Be Problematic?

He can "want" to make money all he wants, but there's an opposing belief system that is actively fighting against his ability to do so.

No matter how hard he works, pushes or tries to make more money — he can't seem to generate the money he wants.

And he won't be able to until he dismantles that belief system.

Is this concept of the power of beliefs becoming more clear to you?

See,

You're ONLY limited by your beliefs. PERIOD.

If you want to expand your results as a man, father, husband and businessman.

You Must FIRST Dismantle Old Beliefs And Expand New Ones.

Why else do you think WarriorBook & The WarriorBrotherhood change so many men's lives?

It's NOT because of my story — everyone has one of those.

It's not because they magically discovered "their WHY" (although it is part of the process)

It's because we've mastered the art and science of liberating men from limiting beliefs using tools like our"Stack"…

…and we have the ability to accelerate results across a man's body, spiritual connection, family and business using productivity systems like our Core-4, One Door & 4 Key's protocols.

But those tools and systems can't expand your beliefs and access your power to produce the specific results you desire until you FIRST…

1. TELL THE FUCKING TRUTH

2. Become aware of the problem holding you back (I call this "The Pit").

3. Understand how we got here as a society of sedated men to begin with.

That's Why I Wrote This Book.

Not so you can learn how to make more money, have more sex and connect more with your wife in the next 90 days than you did in the last 12 months.

That's what the WarriorBook is for…

NOT THIS BOOK.

This is about me meeting you at THE GATE to show you how to unlock it and get access to the path that will ultimately take you where you want to go.

The WarriorBook is THE PATH.

This book, *Be The Man*, opens the gate to the Path.

It begins with the "fucking truth"…

SECTION ONE

THE PIT

*"Through me you go into a city of weeping;
through me you go into eternal pain; through
me you go amongst the lost people."*

—Dante Alighieri

Excerpt from The Inferno, Book One of The Divine Comedy
[Late Middle Ages Italian Poet, 1265-1321]

What LIES Beneath...

New Year's Eve, 2007. As the rest of the world went about celebrating the dawn of a New Year heading into 2008, I lay in my bed, inside my large home that we had acquired not two years before.

My wife sat up next to me and I can still remember the current of wind from the ceiling fan that I had become so addicted to, blowing down upon us.

We had these huge shutters over the left side of some giant windows that filled the master bedroom. I could see the moon reflecting through these giant shades off my wife's face.

She Turned And Looked At Me, With Tears Pouring Down Her Cheeks:

"I didn't Sign Up For This. How are you going to fix it?"

I lay down and put my hands back behind my head, closing my eyes.

My mind raced back to the summer, six months before, of me sharing the stage with Tony Robbins at the Mortgage Planner Summit in Las Vegas,Nevada.

My mortgage empire was expanding and we were dominating, and yet, here I lay, heading into 2008, with everything crumbling around me.

My Marriage Was About To Be Exposed For The Shell That It Was.

What's interesting about the tide is that when it begins to go out, it exposes everything that was hidden.

At low tide, it exposes realities like rocks that you can't see when the tide is high; they're always there, whether you can see them or not.

When the financial tide in my life began to roll out, it exposed a painful reality inside of my life within my marriage, spiritual truth, physical body and business that I had been ignoring for years.

That reality was simply this: my life was not working, but because the money had been so good for so long I was able to simply ignore the painful issues.

The fact was that no matter how much I hustled every single day, my life had become a Sedation Game filled with quicksand that was constantly filling in every single hole that I attempted to dig.

No matter how much I tried to wrap my mind around what was happening, wanting to blame my wife for the pain I was feeling, the loss of all three of my businesses, and the implosion of my entire life, I wouldn't have had my rebirth without it.

This is a critical concept to grasp.

As Men We Have Been Trained To Avoid Pain.

Either by lying, sedating, suppressing or a combination of the three.

However, the act of "Avoidance" is actually what fuels the lies that create more pain which leads to more sedation.

It's A Brutal Cycle With Only One Way Out.

IT BEGINS WITH THE TRUTH.

As painful as it may be to look at the facts and be truthful about them...

As uncomfortable and backwards as it may feel to be vulnerable...

The fact remains,

Everything you desire in this world is on the other side of that pain.

- Confidence

- Self-Worth

- Impact

- Fulfillment

- Connection

- Physical Health

- Spiritual Health

- Financial Wealth

...It's all waiting for you on the other side of the pain.

You Can't Go Around It And There's No Shortcuts.

You must go through it. How?

Well,

We use a tool called **"The Stack"** inside The Warrior's Way to help us identify the truth in any given situation and determine what kind of action is necessary to take, to get what we want.

I share this exact tool and teach the entire system inside **The WarriorBook**

If you already know you need to make a shift in your life, go invest in the book and join the brotherhood NOW by going to http://WarriorBook.com

Reality Bites...

You never hear people shout,

"Hey, you know what? I'm so glad that my life is burning down to the ground right now. I'm so glad I'm selling my bullshit big boy toys that I spent top dollar on so that I can try to put groceries in the fridge and diapers on my babies."

No, that's not the part of the story anybody actually wants to experience, or even acknowledge, let alone write in a book that matters.

They don't want to experience the reality of me sitting in the basement with a bottle of vodka in one hand, drinking myself stupid every afternoon, trying to figure out how in the hell I got here, and how in the hell I was going to get out.

Reality Bites Hardcore When In The Pit.

I reached out to many people while I was in the Pit but most of them simply thought the answer was, "Read this scripture, pray, and life will just work itself out." Although I could appreciate where they were coming from, at the same time it was not assisting me at all.

Day after day,

The Darkness Of Uncertainty Filled My Veins,

slowly killing all creativity and confidence I had.

Inside that pain, the drinking continued and the drugs soon followed.

Because of the stories I lived in at the time, I felt that I couldn't truly expose my reality to anyone and so the cover-ups began.

I would button these exposing parts of myself up every single day as I put my suit jacket on, and I would go out into the world and pretend.

I Pretended That My Life Itself Hadn't Faded Into Oblivion;

that I wasn't hurting. What I didn't realize at the time was that I was slowly committing suicide.

I couldn't see that what I was creating were even greater problems stacked upon the problems I was already facing.

Perhaps as you are reading this book, you might be sitting there with the thought, "Garrett, I don't drink, I don't have marriage problems, my life is really good; I just want *more*."

Or

"Garrett, my life is good, maybe even great, but I'm bored out of my mind and feel like I am about to burn it all to the ground."

Not Thinking Outside of the Burning Box

There are two ends of the same burning wick. You see,

Your Kingdom Can Be Destroyed Equally From One Of Two Directions.

1. Boredom

2. Burn Out

I know it sounds ridiculous to some, but I have watched more men burn their lives to the ground out of boredom when life was good than I have seen men over the years destroy everything because of burnout.

In my life I have experienced both and 2008 was not a Boredom game; it was a Burnout Game.

As my world was burning to the ground, I was left with the greatest challenge that a man faces when shit is not working: Shift.

The "Einstein Method"

You would think that shifting would be easy when something is not working at the level you know it could and should, but the challenge is the fact pointed out by Albert Einstein,

> *"A man's mind lacks the capacity to solve the problems it has created at the same level of thinking that originally created the problem."*

I was stuck.

My mind was closed and I was stuck in a suicide mission of thoughts.

I wanted out of my burning world but I had no idea how to do that, and the possibility of accessing my own liberation based on where my mind was, sat at about zero.

I Was Stuck, I Felt Like A Slave To My Own Mind.

I tried religion, fitness, marriage counseling, talking to my parents; none of it was working.

It seemed to me that I was doomed to a painful death, convinced that I was fast on my path to becoming another Entrepreneurial Statistic of Failure.

When I Fell, Everyone Disappeared And I was All Alone.

The hundreds of people I had employed, all of the individuals I had supported over the years, gone.

There I sat, alone, trying to find the answers in my own insane mind.

- Why does my life hurt so much?

- Why am I so angry?

- Why do I feel so helpless?

- Why do I have all these questions?

- What are all these desires that I am feeling?

There Was No One To Ask; Nowhere I Could Go To Find Answers.

I started searching desperately, trying to find an answer (any answer) that would give me some kind of direction.

After hundreds of conversations with the leaders at church, the individuals in my neighborhood, the people who were supposedly my friends; I started to realize that they were also stuck in many of the same problems that I was,but they lied and suppressed and weren't willing to acknowledge them yet, so our conversations would end up fruitless.

I was so sick of the flat, shallow conversations I was having. **Nobody, it seemed, was willing to talk about *real* Shit**: The Panic, the Pain or the Problems they were facing.

Looking For Support In All The Wrong Places...

"How do I fix this painful reality called my life?" I asked myself.

Unable to find freedom through this internal conversation, I began to blame my wife for everything.

The Blame Game became the easiest move by making my wife a target.

- I blamed her for my pain.

- I blamed her for my confusion.

I told myself a seductive story that supported me in casting her as the character of my destruction.

As I Assaulted My Wife With My Verbal Venom...

...I had become completely ignorant to my role in my own pain.

I ignored the fact that I had shown up like an idiot for almost a decade in our relationship; the more I told myself this insane story that it was all her fault, the more I believed it.

In my darkest pain I was alone. I had no WarriorBook. I had no Brotherhood. I had no Warrior's Way to Having It All.

There was no CODE to live by.

I Was Alone, Frustrated, Hurt And Deeply Confused.

By the end of 2009 I was weighing in at 172 pounds *(I am 6'2" and normally weigh in at a fit 205)* because my solution to all of this pain was to start running every single day.

For most people this would mean a three to five mile jog.

But for me, this meant 20-30 miles every single morning.

I was literally, physically, running myself to death.

I looked sick and unhealthy. I would run and run and drink and drink, trying to find some connection inside of this pain.

Fueled by the story that my wife was the problem and the cause of my pain, I began to search for emotional support from other women in my life since I didn't feel I could get it from her.

Enter My "Rock Bottom"...

I was convinced that another woman was what I needed: one who could love, embrace, and accept me as I was.

This led me to an affair and that's when I finally hit rock bottom.

The day after the Affair, I stood in front of the bathroom mirror, looking into my sunken eyes after returning from a 32 mile run exhausted and ready to go back to bed.

I Couldn't Recognize The Man That Stood In Front of Me.

What had happened to me in less than 18 months? Where was Garrett?

I Wanted To Die.

Some men speak of their affairs as this glorious experience, that they learned a lot and even enjoyed it.

Not me.

Mine was a one-time event, and it was the opposite of everything that my fantasies had told me it would become.

After that experience I felt more alone than I had ever felt in my entire life.

I felt like God had left me just as my wife and family were leaving me.

I was going to fucking lose everything, and for what?

A one-night fling trying to escape who I was.

39

I was convinced that I had become cursed, and that God and the Universe had conspired against me, set out to destroy this shell of a man that I had become because somehow I had missed the turn in the road.

That is, until I heard something.

At The Bottom Of That Painful Pit, All Alone, There Was A Voice That Entered Into My Experience.

It wasn't loud; it just simply said, "Will you listen to me now?"

One of the biggest challenges facing a man in this modern society is the feeling of **BEING ALONE.**

I'll dive into this specific issue a little later in this book.

But I want to point something out.

The deeper I sunk into my pit, the more I felt alone.

The more I felt alone, the more I sedated and suppressed my pain, fear, uncertainty and frustration.

There's A Direct Correlation Between Isolation And Lying.

One of the primary reasons The Warrior Book experience is transformational, is simply because we provide an opportunity for a man to NOT FEEL ALONE.

We give them access to a brotherhood that gives them space to ask questions, get answers and stop living inside their lies.

If you're tired of feeling alone and isolated, confused why you may want something but struggle to actually take action to get it...

Come join us inside the Brotherhood where we're creating breakthrough and implementing the tools and processes from The WarriorBook to get more fit, make more money, have more sex and re-connect with our families.

Come join us...but only if you're committed to doing the work.

It's Not The Size Of The Pit That Matters

I don't know what your Pit looks like:

It could be a small one, or it could be a massive crater like mine was.

- You could be in a situation in which life is painful, or you could be in a situation in which life is just numb.

- You could be in a situation in which life is filled solely with pleasure but you know there's something more out there, and guess what?

Inside of all of that is going to come the same experience for you that I had; at some point, you will need to become humble enough, beaten-down enough, to listen to the Voice inside of you.

On that day, mine said,

"Are You Ready To Listen? Are You Ready To Hear What I Have To Say?"

As I rose from that place, I was very aware that I would likely lose my wife, my family; my everything.

I would become the second-time divorced man, children with two ex-wives, and a walking billboard for "*How To Fuck Up Your Life*, now playing in the douche bag next to you."

The craziest part of these years?

On the outside, everyone thought at some level I was just fine.

I knew I could no longer sustain the lies or the façade.

I refused to continue to maintain the energetic resource necessary to mask, suppress and pretend that I actually believed what I believed in church; that I felt what I felt in life.

I Was Tired Of Pretending And Believing The Lies Inside My Own Mind.

I was sick of being a believer in God; I wanted to Know Him.

I wanted to find and discover my Divinity, but the only way to do this was to have the courage to put my entire life on the line, and in that place, say,

"If I lose it all, that is fine, because I am going to start from a foundation that is built upon Truth."

The Truth May Hurt…But Lies Kill

Little did I realize how difficult this would be, and how much society does not support men like you and I to tell the truth.

Not in business, not in marriage, not in life.

We're Surrounded By People Every Day Who Truly Can't Handle The Full Truth We Have To Share With Them.

These same people have told us to calm down, relax, or tone it down.

- They have asked us to be quiet.

- They have told us to shut up.

- They have demanded that we not share everything even if it means we die.

The world is so politically correct these days that it's almost impossible for a human being to actually express what they are feeling.

For powerful men like you and I, this becomes our downfall.

It becomes our casket.

My life went to the place it went to, my affair happened, all because I couldn't tell the truth to my wife.

- I couldn't speak about how much I was hurting and about how big of a failure I felt like I was.

- I couldn't be honest with her or colleagues in business.

Literally, the Truth would have set me free but I was unable and unwilling to speak it.

How Do You "Be The Man"?

One night, deep inside another fight with my wife, with tears pouring down her cheeks she screamed, **"Just be the man!"** It was the same fight we had every night about the same topics: sex, money, the kids…take your pick.

But in that night's fight, for some reason the phrase she screamed echoed in my soul:

"Just be the man."

The Problem arose in me for the very first time:

"I Don't Even Know What The Fuck 'Be The Man' Means."

Here is the reality:

My dad was never around to teach me how to be a man.

He was gone all of the time providing for the family, and I appreciate his commitment to make sure that we had food and shelter.

But because my Dad was gone all the time, do you know who was teaching me to be a man? My mom.

My mom is a total badass and I love her to death.

I love my dad as well and know he did the very best he could, but he was not an example of what it was to be a whole man in our home.

He was an example of what it was to be a sedated one, a one-dimensional father who could make some money but was not emotionally and physically around.

I Didn't Grow Up With Mentors...

...and guides and examples who truly taught me, "Garrett, this is what it means to be a man."

So, I started looking.

I thought maybe there was somebody who was doing this.

Maybe there could be someone who had figured out how to train me to be a man.

I Googled "how to be a man" (true story) and all kinds of crazy shit came up, none of which had any semblance of what I was truly seeking.

Inside of that, I started searching and reading, going to events and programs, and figured out that part of my problem was that I had not been able to actually see the truth inside of me. I could fundamentally not answer what should seem like the simplest questions in life:

- Who am I beyond the roles of husband? Father?

- Who am I beyond the experience of this religion?

- Who am I beyond this political system?

Beyond All My Labels, Who Was Garrett?

Who am I?

I had no answer for this. I didn't know.

Then I started to have these other conversations enter into my mind.

I went to a workshop where this guy was talking about these 12 categories of life.

I Looked At Him: Fit With A Really Beautiful Wife.

I'm hearing how they talk about sex and intimacy, while I'm sitting in this disconnected relationship in which things are not working out at all with my wife.

I'm looking at them as a couple. They're making money, they're fit, and all of this shit seems to be working in their life.

They've got great kids. I'm like, "Oh my God, they must be full of shit.

There's noway, noway possible, that these 12 areas they talk about could actually be real for them." And yet, they were.

I Wanted To say, "Bullshit," Because It Seemed So Impossible In My Own Life.

I couldn't believe it, yet I deeply wanted it to be true for me also.

And yet, at the beginning of 2018, I launched the Warrior Empire Network, in which the dream that I thought was so unattainable manifesting itself in this couple I had seen in the past was now becoming my reality with the *"Date Your Wife"* podcast.

Seeing my Queen rise in her own world within the hair industry through DKW Styling and Big Money Stylist, the training program behind her hair extension technique known as Natural Beaded Rows (NBR) brought a whole new level to the kind of man I wanted to become as her King.

You might be having the same thoughts.

"Dude, I don't even know if this is possible. Can I truly have it all in my Body, Being, Balance, and Business, Garrett?"

I don't know. It seems like a concept that resonates as truth for me at the Core, but I don't know if that's possible."

If you're like I was, there's likely a part in you that is scrutinizing and part of your mind is listening, just searching…

...for A Reason To Tell Me To Fuck Off.

I wouldn't be upset with you, because guess what my mind would have done? The exact same thing, because when I was in that state of wanting, it seemed so unreal, improbable, and impossible, that I could *have it all*.

The blinders were painfully small through which I saw the world.

See,

My Belief System At The Time Didn't Have The Capacity For Me To See The Possibilities.

My belief system put a limit of the value I gave myself and the skills I believed I was capable of obtaining.

- I just couldn't see it through my world view — so I dismissed it as bullshit.

- I clung to the principles, possibilities and concepts that were small-minded and boring as fuck, but it fit inside my beliefs.

Which is why it took me falling all the way down to rock bottom before I gave myself permission to entertain new perspectives and possibilities.

Maybe that's where you're sitting right now as you read this.

Perhaps the bullshit meter that's rising in your mind is being driven by the stories you believe to be true from a limited belief system.

Again, I get it.

But Here's The Thing, Brother.

If you're reading this book, you're either at rock bottom or you can feel a gravitational pull leading you down in that direction.

Either way,

You must shift to and be open to expanding your belief system to see the possibilities for yourself.

But only if you can tell the truth.

- Only if you're committed to yourself and your family.

- Only if you're ready to choose a brotherhood to support you over lying in isolation.

If you are,

Get a copy of the Warrior Book and join the Brotherhood NOW[2].

---

2   To purchase your copy today, go to: https://warriorbook.com

An Empty Search...

After searching and searching to find this, it came down to one simple truth:

there was no training for what I was seeking.

There was no comprehensive program on what it was to be a man, let alone a four-dimensional modern man facing modern problems in a modern society.

The best that could be delivered up was a series of one-dimensional men who could train you on one, maybe two dimensions.

Most Men That I Have Ever Worked With,

been in business with, or had as clients, were very good at two things: making the money and maintaining their body for the most part.

When it came to spirituality, parenting and marriage, it was a nightmare.

Occasionally I would meet men that were the exception, but across the board there was always at least two areas within his life that he struggled in, pulling the other areas down along with him.

I was like, "Dude, how is it possible that we have defined being a man as a guy who just makes the money?"

That seemed to be the only conversation that was consistent, that the role and goal of "being a man" was to make money.

As long as that happened, sex should follow, and everything else should just take care of itself. Yet this was not my experience because I had made the money and still was left wanting:

I Knew That It Was A Lie.

So I Went On A Journey To Figure Out Why.

Along the way, I uncovered something so massive it was hard to believe at first.

My reality, which was what most modern men were facing, had been manufactured over 100 years ago to systematically destroy mankind by sedating the Kings.

The results of living we were experiencing today had come on the wake of a series of world-altering shifts over a century that made it almost impossible for men like you and I to ever have it all.

My Brother, All Great Revolutions Began With A Simple Question.

My question was,

"How In The Hell Did We Get Here As Men?"

Waiting Will Get You Killed

Would you advise a man with Cancer to "Wait" until his body is shriveling up before he goes to get treatment?

The obvious answer is NO, right?

It would cost him his life if you did. Brother,

Consider this…

Why would your marriage be any different?

Why would the relationship with your kids be any different?

Isn't your family just as important to you as LIFE is to a man with cancer?

So why wait?

Especially when the solution is sitting right in front of you for $100.

Invest in the book[3] and come join me and the rest of the men in the Warrior Brotherhood.

---

3   Go to https://warriorbook.comto secure your copy.

ONCE THIS MISSION IS ACCOMPLISHED,
YOUR NEXT STEP IS TO SECURE:

WARRIORBOOK

A MODERN MAN'S GUIDE TO HAVING IT ALL
IN BODY, BEING, BALANCE & BUSINESS

SECTION TWO

THE PAINFUL PROBLEM

"The Industrial Revolution has two phases: one material, the other social; one concerning the making of things, the other concerning the making of men."

—Charles A. Beard

[Influential American historian
in first half of 20th century, 1874-1948]

Born Into Sedation...

As much as I wanted to blame my dad for not raising me to be a man, the truth was, my father (like me) had been born into a Game of Sedation that had been gaining momentum for generations before he was born.

The SEDATION GAME Was Created Long Before My Father And I Were Born,

spinning out of control, taking men from a place of power and thrusting them into a place of powerlessness.

This dark system was literally destroying kings and turning them into peasants.

By the time my father was born, this was all the men around him knew.

He didn't understand the disconnect behind why, how, or what he was experiencing and feeling.

The last thing in the world he was able to do was to actually talk with anybody about it. Why had this happened?

See,

I wanted to know and understand how we as men had gotten here. Every man I looked around at, and came into conversation with, far and few between were those who were willing to beat the drum the way that I believe a four-dimensional modern man living the Warrior's Way should.

The Uphill Battle...

Living in Power as a man these days is almost impossible with the current set up of rules and guidelines that we are supposed to follow according to what society has dictated.

There is an epidemic of disconnected teenagers and men in their 20s and 30s who are literally becoming dysfunctional at everyday living of the most basic human skills.

This problem is not only apparent in the younger generations, but is showing itself in massive ways for men who are in their 40s and 50s, with suicide rates that have gone through the roof for men in their 60s.

Divorce Rates Are Running Rampant...

...as men scramble to try to figure out "How to Be the Man" while women grow tired of the pussies their husbands have become and would rather raise their children alone *and* fulfill both roles as Mother and Father than to be married to deadwood.

There's an alarming rise of divorces that we're experiencing inside of the United States being filed by women in their 50s: the moment the kids graduate from high school and move out, they look at the man they have tolerated for nearly three decades and say,

"Forget you, my kids are out of the house so I'm out of here to finally live my life."

Men are left hollow and alone, and don't know why because they were acting like what they thought a man was **supposed** to act like.

The truth is, there are tons of programs that help women, but when was the last time you saw one to help men?

It didn't exist. I couldn't find one, which is why I launched Wake Up Warrior in 2012. Prior to that, I uncovered the facts about the Systematic Sedation of Men including the **why** and **how** it happened.

I discovered that history can teach us more about our own lives and how to course correct them when things are off than what I ever imagined.

Solving Systematic Sedation

In order to understand how my dad and I got to this place (and how you did too), we've got to go back to the late 1800s and early 1900s, on into the beginning of what became known as the Industrial Revolution.

There was a fundamental shift in the way that living occurred here inside of the United States and around the world at this time.

The Shift Would Affect Everyone...

...and literally change the way the world worked.

Before the Industrial Revolution, the majority of society existed in what has been labeled an agrarian existence.

This way of living occurred in the following reality: Dad, mom, and child co-creating together.

They were feminine and masculine equals, yet at the same time distinct and different in their roles with the man as the head of the household.

A typical day for Dad would be waking up in the morning then going to work on the farm minutes from the house and at the core of his Community.

Guess who also got to watch and participate in this same work every single day?

Johnny.

Little Johnny would go to work with his dad side by side, literally, every single day.

"How Do I Be A Man?"

Little Johnny was seeing through example on how being a man worked.

Dad didn't disappear for the day and then return home to guide the children at night.

From breakfast to lunch to dinner, dad was actively role modeling to children respect, education, hard work, fear of God, connection to the queen, respect and responsibility.

Every single day, dad was demonstrating to his sons the answer to the question, How Do I Be A Man?

That same question is still asked today, yet a massive shift in mentality led to a different answer.

What does this have to do with the Industrial Revolution? Everything, my friends.

Then The Industrial Plague Attacked Society...

See...

Until the 1800s, the majority of society lived in self-sufficiency this way.

There was a co-parenting relationship: Dad and Mom worked together in the home.

There was this home-base Core Connection where family mattered and was valued, where each individual knew his and her role in running a household and land.

This way of thinking and living had been a part of society for centuries, so surely a cataclysmic event caused this great shift in thinking,right?

It did, a plague came about, but not as a natural disaster.

The Promise of More caused us as a society to shift from this agrarian age in which mom and dad co-parented and co-raised the children to one of limitless possibilities.

The "Big Promise" That Changed The World...

The Industrial Age offered up a Big Promise.

The promise itself was an interesting one, very appealing to Mom and Dad.

How do we know?

Because it changed the entire world from what it was to the way that we know it now.

Some people feel it was a bad, horrible, and an awful promise that caused the rich to grow richer and the poor to grow poorer.

Although the rapid growth of industrialization did have its upsides in building a powerhouse nation in America, the downside as to what this did to the family was hard to ignore.

The Industrial Revolution Wasn't Seen As A Problem; It Was A Solution To A Problem.

With that solution came a "cost" many were willing to pay, which also brought with it a new series of problems that we could not have anticipated. This is the crazy catch-22 part of all blessings: we can't have them without the downside curse of natural consequences.

So, what was the solution to the problem?

The Industrial Pitch was essentially this: MOVE in order to progress forward. Literally, let go of the Farm and move your family from the country to the city.

No more blood, sweat and tears with the back-breaking work of the farm.

No seasonal issues with weather, or dealing with a starving family if the crops failed.

Men were enticed to venture forth into the new possibilities awaiting them within the city with more certainty in the future there for what?

The Temptation Of Money!

All at the low cost of simply leaving the home during the day for the factory and office.

Instead of Dad working side by side with little Johnny, he would be required to leave the home every morning, travel miles away and go to work in the factory, a place that Little Johnny would not be allowed to work side by side with his father.

It was no longer a possibility to have hands-on schooling side by side while performing chores and working on the farm with dad, but that felt like a justifiable loss in order to give the family more, right?

What had not been considered along with this commute was the distance between this separate place of work and home, and that's where several other things began to shift in men.

Before The Industrial Game,

Dad was rewarded for playing the Game of Life on the farm by using his creativity, innovation, and ability to solve problems.

This game was worked out of a man with rote actions specific for one job.

Men were punished in the marketplace for innovation because there was a systematic way of doing things that were not to be disrupted.

He Was Required To Sell His Crown For Cash,

Taken from his position as a king and compelled to become a cog in a machine.

Brother,

You may not be experiencing the exact working environment as men did back then.

However,

The principle of"the systematic way of doing things" is all around us.

The rigid box we get placed in as men who are supposed to have all the answers, show no emotions, never get vulnerable and repress anything that doesn't fit inside the narrow box.

This dynamic inherently makes a man feel alone.

They squeeze a man inside a box whether he fits in it or not, then they give him rules that say "you're not allowed to show your frustration" of not fitting in or even question anything about the box.

Then they frame everything outside the box as "weak," "soft," "violent," "too aggressive," "too loud" and soon.

As a result, we have…

...A Society Of Men Who Are Experiencing The Same Pain,

confusion, frustration and lack of authenticity...yet nobody is willing to step up against it.

Most don't even realize the problem stems from the manufactured BOX and frame to begin with.

And so we sit alone, isolated in our game trying to figure out "what's wrong" and "how can I hide this side of me."

The only answer we have is sedation with porn, video-games, work, social media, pills, weed, alcohol, etc.

Inside The WarriorBook,

We give you the tools to break free from all forms of sedation as well as the strategies and frameworks to show you how to live your life on a daily basis in a way where you don't even experience the need to sedate from anything at all.

It's one thing to stop doing the shit you really don't want to be doing (as is the case with most addictive behavior),

But it's a whole other thing to give a man access to power that removes the very part of his life that is driving him to want to sedate in the first place.

That's REAL transformation.

And that's what's happening daily inside of the brotherhood.

Are you ready to join us?[4]

From Kings To Tools

A significant percentage of males in society went from being a king in the home, praised with admiration by his children and his wife, where the family unit all worked alongside each other, to a disposable tool.

Sometimes he would not even see the sun as he would leave for work early in the morning, enter the office while it was still dark, returning home late after long factory hours and commuting after sunset.

An Exhausted Reality...

On the odd nights that this industrial man got home before Little Johnny was asleep, he was so exhausted from the relentless grind that any attempt to fulfill a role as a father was mediocre at best in such a fatigued state.

He Still Wanted To Be There For His Kids,

but little by little as he started to climb the corporate ladder towards the Industrial Revolution's American

---

4   Go to https://warriorweek.comand fill out an application to join Warrior Week.

Dream, priorities shifted more and more from the influence he once had while on the farm.

All of this was justified under the belief that the money was the most important gift he could offer his children: a future brighter than his own with opportunity to experience a "better" and easier life.

What didn't he account for, however?

The time he was gone from little Johnny and the impact of having mom fulfill both the Father and Mother roles meant that little Johnny wasn't learning how to be a man *by* a man.

Dad thought in his mind that at least they weren't living in tenements like some oft he immigrants that had come over from the Motherland where the whole family had to work.

There Was More Money,

so mom and the kids were actually having the opportunity within the city to experience some things they didn't get to experience out on the farm.

They wore better, tailored clothes made from textile mills, and eventually moved up into a better house.

But doing this the family gained more social networks, friends and opportunities Dad looked at this overall experience as good.

At least from the outside this is how it appeared. "This was beautiful," he decided.

Slowly, though, the game was different, and Mom shifted as well, saying, "It's okay, Love. I know you're tired. You're doing everything you can to provide for this family."

Over One Generation Span (around 20 years) Boys Were No Longer Working Side By Side With Father Anymore.

They were no longer being raised by both parents.

They had a father who only saw them for one hour, maybe two, at night; this is what they saw and sot hey figured that's how it's to bed one.

It became the norm to be raised by Mother.

This may not seem like a big deal, but just like all journeys that we take, If we shift just one degree, we soon split and head into a completely different direction.

Look how quickly thousands of years of fatherhood had shifted within just one to two generations as the agrarian life was replaced by the factory and office life:

In The Beginning, It Doesn't Really Look Like Too Much.

After all, our whole purpose in life is supposed to lead towards progress and expansion,right?

And that's exactly what the Industrial Age and Progressive Era consisted of.

This simple shift declared, "Fathers, your job is to be a cog and bring home the bacon.

Become a tool of production by being a cog in a system, inside the factory of the Industrial Revolution; that's how you hunt the buffalo now."

Not a king with council to provide for your family the emotional, financial, social, spiritual support that you were once required to live and teach.

That's outdated.

Now we just need you to go produce in the office:

"Go, Make The Money."

The Progressive Era then came in to rectify the unsafe and unlawful working conditions, but any thought on the mental progress of the working man became even more sedated.

71

And Then It Got Worse...

…Part of that was due to outside events, when the world experienced a Great War to end all wars, which further solidified this mentality that man serves society best by being away from the home.

We had all of these boys that saw their Dad working in the factory and office become men as soldiers in World War I, learning first hand in the trenches further "progress" that war brings.

A nation-wide Depression occurred as we were slowly reminded that it requires hard work to bring in the paycheck within an office or factory, but because jobs were so few, men didn't know what to do.

Countries were invaded and declared war on others as World War II then ensued, providing drafts and opportunities for men to continue to go out and not only provide for their family, but for their nation's freedoms and liberties.

In The Military, There Is No Room For Feelings.

We needed to take those feelings and suppress them because they'll get in the way of killing another man.

Now, men have been killing each other since Cain found a rock, so none of that was new; what was new was that war had been created with industrial strength, and it required industrial men to execute it.

To defend the truths that we hold self-evident here in the United States of America, men declared,

"We've All Got To Go Fight The Wars Of Old Men."

So, Johnny who was disconnected from Dad already, has now learned to shut his feelings down.

Entire generations of men were taught that their role was to not only hunt the buffalo, but at the same time, to not even feel.

Feeling anything was not safe because you could die if you did, and so this global lie became truth.

The message became:

Feeling
+
Showing Emotion
=
Death

So if you want to live, operate like a machine and act on what you're told, not how you feel.

This created what we have come to know in society as The Greatest Generation.

It's also created an expectation that still haunts men today that emotions and feelings need to be filtered through the "acceptable"strainer.

As a result you have a society that basically says,

"those feelings are ok, but those ones…you need to shut those down."

One of the first concepts we dive into inside The WarriorBook is the power and leverage you gain from emotions.

Remember,

I briefly touched on this earlier.

The Fastest And Most Effective Way To Achieve Big-ass Results, Is By Taking Big-Ass Action.

But here's the thing.

Emotions and feelings drive those actions.

Before you decide to finally get back in shape, chances are, it's the emotions that were triggered by seeing the number on the scale or looking at old pictures when you used to befit.

Without accepting those emotions, there is no action.

So when society puts a limit on what we're allowed to show and feel emotionally, we tend to avoid things that may trigger us to feel those emotions.

Why do you think men avoid the doctors?

Because it may trigger them to find out some bad news that makes them feel out of control, vulnerable and weak.

So They Avoid It All Together Even If It Means Dying.

Men refuse to have the difficult conversations with their wives because they don't want to go down the path of potentially exposing some truths about themselves and their marriage that makes them feel out-of-control and confused.

So they avoid it.

Even if it means divorce or infidelity.

The list of examples could go on and on. The point is,

There Are Massive Amounts of Power inside

"Feelings" and "Emotions."

But you must give yourself permission to extract the power by entering into certain conversations and be willing to expose facts that you know will elicit emotions that society has deemed unacceptable for you to feel.

A Big Reason Why Men Inside The Brotherhood Experience Such Accelerated Results...

...is simply because we teach them through the WarriorBook how to leverage difficult conversations and leverage their emotions in a systematic way to produce results.

We do this every day within our "STACK" protocol.

Where it takes some men years to make small shifts in their marriage or business from avoiding everything they need to see or experience to light a fire under them,

We attack every day.

This is why it's become clockwork to see men get more results in all 4 areas of their life in 90 days than they do in one area from the previous 24 months.

Grab a copy of The WarriorBook[5] if you're ready to experience this time-warp for yourself.

---

5   https://warriorbook.com

The Greatest Generation

While the men were gone to War, the women were back on the Home front, trying to figure out their new place in this new Age.

Society still had to continue, after all.

For the first time inside the United States, we began to see a significant rise inside the capacity of employment for women.

Women Replaced The Men who were called out to war in the factories AND were still required to raise the children.

I'm going to have you consider that these events could have gone a different way in bringing the family structure back to where it was less than 50 years earlier, but instead, this then led to its own movement for women, shifting roles within society which we will discuss in a few moments.

Mixing the Industrial Mindset with the War Mindset, entire generations of men were told to stop feeling, stay disconnected and don't you dare show any feelings or fucking bitch about how you might feel inside.

Just get the job done.

Don't talk about your feelings, don't talk about your emotions.

Men Were Taught Not To Feel.

That being a man means you go get shit done regardless of how you're feeling at the time.

You come home, and you don't bitch about it.

You don't talk about it and you don't get emotional about it.

You Hold This Stoic Position Of Emotionless Power.

In doing that, you are a great man.

That was my grandfather, Colonel in the Air Force for 30 years:

Beautiful, powerful man.

However, in the final years of his life here on this planet, the truth started to come out about the pain of what it was to be him; how hard it was for him to Be The Man society told him to be.

And yet, for his entire life he had been taught, trained, and educated not to be real, raw and emotional with his wife, his kids or his grandchildren.

He literally stayed in the Game of War that feelings could get him killed.

When he came back for his last 30 years, he didn't know how to operate any other way but Focused Fire on the outside with a Chaotic Emotional Circus occurring on the inside.

Twisting Feminism With The Feminist Movement

And then in the 1960s things inside the United States began to take another massive shift.

From finally gaining the right to vote in 1920, women created a small door and opened it slightly during World War II as men who were fighting in the war were replaced by women in the workforce, but it was the '60s and '70s that this Feminist Movement door fully swung open.

Inside was a twisted, bastardized version of the feminist suffragists which declared:

"We Don't Need Men."

We're not just equal, we're superior and they are unnecessary. We can do for ourselves anything that a man can do for us."

What started inside offeminism with votes for women and this first declaration at the door that said,

"We want to have a voice…"

then shifted to the twisted feminist version which threw that door off its hinges with "We want our voice to scream out the equality we demand because we are the same."

Equality became: we are the same, and in being the same we don't need you.

Depolarization of Couples

This became the Giant Rift, a depolarization of couples;

Men who were now having to compete with masculine energy with their women and intimacy was slowly being replaced with Competition.

Thoughts in Dad's mind started to become,

> *"It's hard enough that I have to go fight these assholes all day at the office. I then have to come home and battle for a voice inside my own home. I can't talk about my feelings anywhere because society told me I'm not supposed to in order to be a man. I already feel emasculated and castrated because I'm married to a feminist. I'm not sure what I'm supposed to do."*

Let's clarify what it means to be the same by recognizing what isn't:

A Penis And A Vagina Will Never Be The Same Thing.

A woman and a man are not the same thing. They never will be.

I don't care if you're gay or straight or whatever the hell your fucking sexual orientation is: There is Woman and there is Man.

They are not the same.

They are equal, but they will never fucking be the same.

One Is Not Superior To The Other.

This became another subtle insertion of a lie into our society as masculine traits of hunting buffalo began to rise in women and men began to get confused at levels they'd never been confused in before.

How do I actually show up as the man when I'm confused about what being the man means?

Many men think, "I'm looking at this woman but she's kind of being the man, showing up like a dude right now."

Confusion Is Running Rampant For Men Because It's Completely Misidentified.

We don't even know what being a man *is* anymore because everywhere we turn,men are being disappointed, disjointed, and disconnected.

They're being told,"

- Shut up, go get the money,

- don't talk about your feelings,

- and just so you know, we don't need you because we're the same."

The Confusion Age?

What quantifies this at an even bigger level? The Information Age.

This technological boom began in the late 1990s and then took off into warp drive after the early 2000s.

For the first time ever, information proliferated globally through the World Wide Web, where information was no longer only found in books but at the ease of our fingertips.

Men and women began to search out insight through the onslaught of information as it became mobile through cell phones and various electronic devices within a few short years.

And Yet, All Of This Unlimited Access To Information Was drowning Us.

Men and women were searching for answers only to receive contradictory opinions masked as fact; that if it's posted on the internet, it *must* be true.

You Think That Information Will Liberate You, When It Has Actually Enslaved You.

We are becoming robots, plugged into various electronic devices day in and out.

Five to six generations later from the men that left the agrarian lifestyle…

Boys are being born into a world that makes no sense.

The lessons from these past generations of men and information doesn't liberate us, nor does it address the fact that we now have 75 plus years of patterns being built and ingrained.

Boys Never Becoming Men

This confusion has become something known by psychiatrists as "extended adolescence."

Divorce rates are running rampant (if a couple even chooses to marry) and we have more single moms with children than we have ever had in our planet's history.

As we've been able to vaccinate certain diseases that plagued society, we now have super viruses, more physical disease and dysfunction than we have ever had.

More Disappointment And Exodus From Religion Than We Have Ever Experienced.

More governments being toppled and confusion inside of political regimes than we have ever seen.

Information has not made all things better, despite what the marketing claims.

Information has merely accelerated the inevitability of the implosion in the world as we know it.

Inside of all of this there's this exposed reality of boys who are staying boys long into their 30s and 40s now, never leaving home.

They're saying, "You know what? I don't know how to even play this Game called adulthood let alone know how to win.

I Don't Know What It Is To Be A Man. Nobody Is Teaching Me.

The men I see on reality television, YouTube, and social media are not teaching me.

Governments and political officers aren't teaching me how to be a man.

Everyone's getting divorced. Nobody is staying married.

Families are becoming smaller yet blended.

The entire landscape of making money is changing.

This Game Called "Being A Man" is a Goddamn Nightmare.

Inside this confusion, single and divorced men simply choose to Not Grow Up.

And why would they?

What incentive is there except the miserable life that they saw their fathers live?

"Eat, drink and be merry for tomorrow we die", has become the mantra of the Modern Boy Man who has forgotten he is a King.

Hell, at 30-40 years old, if you can still run around like a 22-year-old frat boy, play **World of Warcraft**® every single night and **Call of Duty**® on your gaming system, get laid with women that are 5-10 years younger than you, and consume an unlimited amount of porn, why in the world would you want to grow up and move out of your parent's basement?!

Shifting the Foundation of Our Society

The Foundation of our society is driven by kings, By Men.

The way they lead nations comes down to how they lead from the inside of their own families, and that family dichotomy is being destroyed.

The boys that are being born into the Game have been given no clear path and so they choose to remain boys.

Where does this lead?

A society that no longer wants to raise families.

Pornography and quick promises of sex on social media platforms like Tinder have replaced any attempt to work on lasting relationships, because that requires work.

And a lot of it! This is a time of NOW, not working towards something in the long run.

Over 35 percent of all content consumed on the web is pornographic in nature by men, so why are they buying porn?

Why are they masturbating daily? Why is this occurring?

Because Men Are Lost Without A Roadmap.

They have no idea what it is to truly be a man. And it is not their fault.

The message has become so confused with the only maps women have to offer titled "Read My Mind" or "Be the Man" which when opened has no Key to decipher the content inside.

Women are not to blame in all of this either. They are simply playing the Game they were also taught.

Trying to play two sides of the equation, the first as the old school tactic of being a woman which says "Be the Man" to their masculine counterparts yet even they don't know what that fucking means; they just know it's what they need.

And then there's the other side of the equation, in which most of these women have become just as confused as men about what it actually means to be feminine resulting in a daily emotional castration of "is it on or off?" with the man they are with.

Nobody in society seems to have the Key to the MAP.

This is why my marriage was plummeting to divorce.

Some people were like, "Well, that's because you cheated, dumbass" which is definitely part of the equation in my own life.

My Life was plummeting to divorce because neither one of us had an answer on what it meant to "Be the Man."

Do you think my dad had an answer? No.

Do You Think My Church Leaders Had An Answer?

No!

Their answer was, "Pray to God." Nice. Fuck off.

I appreciate your little Sunday School answer but it's not cutting it.

It's not cutting it with me nor with any of the thousands of men that I'm engaged with on this topic every single week.

Finding the Definition of "Being A Man"

We needed something *more*.

What even is the definition of a man pursuing a life of having it all?

We knew what the one-dimensional man looked like: go make some money and workout.

Hopefully inside of that you can get laid a couple of times so you feel good about yourselves.

If your wife doesn't want to put out, no problem.

Porn is just a few mouse clicks away and you can just jack off for free without making any deposits.

If that doesn't cut it, then you'll cheat.

Inside of this, men were left with no guidance system at all.

This isn't about women attacking, being wrong, or doing something stupid. Women were just as oblivious in the Game as we were (though we'd never tell them that).

Our Entire Society Is Now Plummeting Into Chaos Because Kings—MEN—Are Not Leading.

Men are not standing.

How is terrorism running rampant?

Because even our political systems are not being led by kings anymore.

Sedated jerks hold the seats.

What runs rampant inside our body when it is not healthy? A virus.

Cancer cells become activated and begin to build without us even realizing it.

We are getting destroyed from the inside out, both male and female. It's happening everywhere.

Everywhere.

When I saw this, I realized it wasn't even our fault.

I was sharing this information with a friend one day and I was like,

> *"Dude, we're all messed up. I don't even know what we are supposed to do with this. How do we fix this?"*

My friend responded,

"Well, Why Don't *You* *F*ix It?"

"Pffft."

Feeling a lot like most leaders do when it comes to attacking a giant problem, I questioned my capabilities and capacities:

- Who am *I* to do this?

- Who am I to be great and lead this movement?

- Who am I to start this conversation and define what a man is?

- What a Modern Warrior Man is?

If Not You, Then Who?

A question worth an answer.

Long before society started questioning my validity of who I am, and whether or not I'm qualified, I was asking myself those questions.

Who Am I To lead?

I've burned a lot of shit to the ground.

Why not somebody who at least has their shit together?

The Warrior's Way Revolution

Pick one of the clean cut guys. I'm a bit of a maniac. Why me? Why me?!

"Listen dude, if it's not you, then who?" If not you, then who?

"Who is more qualified thana guy who has genuinely fucked everything up, to build the map on the way out of the Gates of Hell to the Place of Power?

You speak about this 'have it all' situation, but you don't have it. So why don't you figure out how to build it?"

This one idea began a Revolution.

When I looked around at the results in our society on one dimensionality training, what I saw were men who were alone, depressed, hiding,sick, suffering, struggling, hurting, confused, frustrated, suicidal, homicidal, addicted, dying, and alone.

I knew what it was like because I have felt all of those things as well.

I took that on and said,

"If It's Not Me, Then Who?"

I don't know who else it could be, so I'm going to give it a shot. Not to lead other's lives. No. I just want to liberate mine.

"Out-Of-Body" Advice

Step outside of your own head for a minute and consider the advice you would give yourself.

[You] "I'm tired of hesitating to launch my big idea and sick of settling for crumbs when I know I should be feasting…I know I'm just stuck in my head and paralyzed by procrastination and uncertainty…I'm also aware of a **system** and powerful group of men who can help me **"escape average"** and step into **ELITE STATUS** where I know I belong…And the investment is$100."

What would you say to that?

"Don't even worry about it bro, everything is going to work out just the way you want if you just keep waiting."

Fuck NO.

My highly educated guess is that you would want to slap the shit out of yourself for not seeing the ONLY choice.

ONCE THIS MISSION IS ACCOMPLISHED,
YOUR NEXT STEP IS TO SECURE:

WARRIORBOOK

A MODERN MAN'S GUIDE TO HAVING IT ALL
IN BODY, BEING, BALANCE & BUSINESS

GO TO **WARRIORBOOK.COM**

SECTION THREE

THE POSSIBILITY

*"But when a long train of abuses and
usurpations, pursuing invariably the same
Object evinces a design to reduce them under
absolute Despotism,
it is their right it is their duty,
to throw off such Government, and to provide
new Guards for their future security."*

—Declaration of Independence

Collisions And Conflicts...

A worldview is nothing more than viewing the world from a place that what we believe is real to us.

It doesn't mean that World is actually real to anybody else; it just means it's real to us.

97

Now, can you and I be influenced by the world around us and the world views of people around us?

Absolutely.

Are We Affected By This With Social Media?

Absolutely.

Are we affected by this with television and the churches that we go to?

Absolutely.

The people that you associate with more often than not are the people who share a common worldview with you.

Most of us do not spend time with somebody who has a conflicting worldview because when you have two opposing worldviews, they collide and cause conflict. One Of The Great Demises Inside Of This "Sedated Man Experience"

- Conflict itself has become something that is politically incorrect

- I shouldn't actually take a stand for a new worldview or the truth the way I see it

- Ultimately, unless you collapse yourself down into the politically correct worldview, then it's impossible for you to actually be accepted.

- Most men find it significantly easier to surrender their opinion about the world that they want and just collapse it down into the worldview of what is, not recognizing that in doing so they are continuing the insanity to the next generation.

At Some Point YOU MUST TAKE A STAND.

A Stand just like the Founding Fathers of the United States of America who said to British Rule,

Founding Father Bad Asses

"You know what?

Your taxes are too high.

We don't want to be part of this sovereignty anymore.

We don't support your worldview about how we should live here in this country, nor do we support your governance anymore.

We're going to create a document called the Declaration of Independence.

We're going to unroll it and sign this bitch, all of us together."

This small band of men, prominent leaders only within their own communities and not yet known to the Crown, knew they were committing high treason putting this document together.

And yet, they proceeded in signing it like the wig-wearing bad asses they were, declaring their independence, liberating themselves from what the English crown thought to be true.

They said,

We Declare Our Independence.

Our worldview is free of the worldview that you say is true.

We reject that worldview.

Not only that, we pledge our lives, our liberty, and our fortunes upon this land to say 'Fuck you' and your worldview."

Well, they were a little more eloquent than that, but the feeling behind the declaration hasn't changed.

Where are the men willing to make declarations like that today? Do they still even exist?

These were men of integrity; men who listened to the Voice inside of them, willing to take a stand and be comprehensive men.

That passion to be willing to commit a treasonous act so that others may be free is hard to come by in leadership after a century of the systemized sedation of men.

What We Have Ended Up With Is A Bunch Of Weak Boys;

Men Who Never Grew Up, That Cannot Take A Stand.

Social Media Opinions; It's Not Working

Social media and the internet has given every asshole an opinion.

"Keyboard Vigilantes" run rampant around the world. Disconnected, unconscious assholes whose opinion, in some twisted reality, some actually think matters.

All of a sudden, we have become influenced in our worldview by people that we don't know, who we don't give a shit about, and yet their opinions are dictating our lives.

The Media World Has Become A Den Of Thieves And A Band Of Liars.

Social Media is forming our Worldview every single day, in some of the most twisted and distorted ways.

In some ways, it is beautiful and in others it is destroying us and everything that we hold dear.

So the question I have for you is this,

"Is Your Life Working?"

If it is, then the Worldview you are living through is working and you can continue living the way you are with no issue.

But…if your life is not working and you are searching for more, then you are left with only one reality:

CHANGE YOUR WORLD VIEW.

Damn straight.

The only solution is to destroy the worldview that guided you to create the reality that you desire to change.

Figuratively speaking, it is time for you to sign your own Declaration of Independence that compels you to no longer live as a man that society has decided to tax us with by declaring,

"I will no longer live the one to two-dimensional lifestyle as a sedated modern peasant king who lives in the shack and rejects his crown.

I reject this doctrine, and I say, 'Fuck you, world doctrine. Fuck you, century of tradition. Fuck you, political correctness. Fuck *you*.' **I choose to live.**"

Here's a key concept I want you to sink your teeth into.

Warrior Is NOT Another Box To Fit Inside.

There's men of different faiths, beliefs, sexual orientation and political affiliations inside the Brotherhood.

I'm not saying you need to adopt my worldview.

I'm not saying you need to adopt the worldview of any of the brothers inside the Brotherhood.

What I am saying is, you must find the worldview that serves you and ultimately gets you the life you want.

Whatever That Is, Is Up To You.

Sure,

We have Codes we live by and tools we use to execute the systems and strategies from the WarriorBook.

But it's all there to serve YOU and your family.

Not me or anyone else.

See,

After you join the Brotherhood,

You'll quickly see that our worldviews, stories, past pain and experiences all differ.

The Thing That Binds Us Together Is The Pursuit Of Having It All.

It's being sick and tired of living life on the sidelines and showing up as sedated and suppressed versions of ourselves.

It's sick of playing small in business...

...Sick of feeling sluggish and sloppy

Sick of fear holding us back from creating big shit.

And it's the fact that we're all DOING SOMETHING ABOUT IT.

What say you?

I know you're sick of all the same things we were too.

But are you willing to do something about it?

If you are, grab a copy[6] of the WarriorBook and join us as we build kingdoms, connect with our queen and children...and "have it all."

What Does Living Mean?

---

6   You can secure your copy by going to https://warriorbook.com

But What Does Living As A Modern Man Mean?

What is the current world's view of a Modern WarriorKing?

You see, I had to begin to define this inside my own life.

I didn't start doing this because I knew you existed, or saw a Revolution ahead of me that was going to change millions of families' lives.

What I saw was a life that wasn't working, and it was mine: *my* life was not working.

My Worldview Was Destroying Me And I Had To Change Or Die.

To hell with anybody else;

I wanted to wake up with a Desire to live and I knew this was going to require me to change the world I saw.

So, what does it mean for me to ultimately have it all?

What do I want my life to look like? What do I want as a man?

I want to feel Harmony, waking up in the morning and mentally feeling like I am on fire.

As an athlete, I had moments, even after my athletic career was over, where my body felt just like a weapon, which exuded this powerful confidence because of the way I was eating and the way I was training my body.

There Was This Confidence That Seemed To Affect Everything Else Around Me.

- I also wanted to feel like God and I were on the same page, fucking tattoos and all.

- I wanted to feel like I could hear the Voice inside of me, that as soon as I woke up,

- I knew my life mattered because this Higher Source, this power called God, this Universe around me, confirmed that it did.

But, you know what? That's not enough.

- I looked into my home and saw the relationship with my wife and children, and said,

I Wanted To Be Done With All This Guilt And Shame.

- I want to be done with these inabilities to communicate and be honest; when I'm fired up,I want to be able to speak my truth, and when my wife is fired up, to be able to allow her to speak her truth as well.

- I needed to learn how to communicate and be real inside that relationship.

- I needed to learn how to be a parent: babies don't come with goddamn instruction manuals.

I wish they did.

Confused As A Husband...

Sexuality, spirituality, communication and intimacy inside of a relationship are all categories within marriage, yet I realized I didn't know how to be a husband.

These topics were all a blur to me and I had no true map to make them work at any level.

I Came To A Very Clear Reality That I Didn't Know How To Be A Husband.

I seriously did not know. It was the greatest and craziest day of my life when I came to truly realize:

"I don't even know how to be a husband; I've been trained by disconnected, sedated men. I don't even know what it looks like to be a husband my wife wants at her side."

I grew up seeing men who would come in after being gone all day golfing on a Saturday, and feel entitled to dinner ready right at the time he walked through the door...

...food on the table with the kitchen already cleaned...

and then sit down on his throne, the couch, to watch football, waiting for the dinner bell to ring.

Then, he'd rise up from one throne to the next one,

Eating As The Fucking Lord Of The Land At The Head Of The Table.

and promptly leave the food and plates to go back to the lounge chair, watching more football on TV while the women cleaned.

These men would talk and play pool, and then they would go to their royal bed chambers, still entitled as a king.

If they felt like they needed to get laid, the wife better perform her marital duties.

This was the example I was being given...what I saw happening all around me.

Now, there is absolutely nothing wrong with playing golf, watching football on Sunday, having your wife cook for you or SEX.

I especially enjoy that last part.

But what I saw behind these actions was an unconscious series of patterns that were creating marriages filled with Suppression and Secrets.

A vast majority of the marriages I saw like this were ending in divorce or worse; complete apathy.

Looking For The Man I Knew I Needed To Be

So the question is:

Who are the role models to follow on how to be a man?

A husband and a father?

Most of us were not raised with fathers who taught us this.

Infact, we are now experiencing generations of men who were raised in fatherless homes.

We Were Not Trained On How To Be The Man That We Knew We Needed To Be.

I knew I had to take my responsibility as a father in a completely different direction than I had seen my father take with me, or how my grandfather had approached fatherhood with him.

I knew I needed to be a better lover and a more seductive player inside of my wife's life.

I needed to be more supportive, emotionally available, and able to communicate better.

I needed to be able to allow her space to grow and become, yet not be triggered by my own ego when doing it.

109

I knew I needed to find a relationship with God, but I was so stuck in my religious patterns I was raised with that I couldn't get it; it didn't make any sense to me.

I couldn't connect inside that space, and so I had to ask myself better questions that ultimately had me leave the church.

I Knew I Needed To Make Money, But I Also Refused To Build Businesses That I Didn't Feel Had Made A Difference.

Not that the mortgages, insurance and financial services that I came from had no value and importance; I just wanted to create and build businesses that mattered.

I didn't want to be a capitalist for capitalism's sake. I wanted to have it all, but I didn't knowhow.

One day I was talking with some friends about this concept of "having it all" and I shared with them,

"Well, I think we could be fit, I think we can be spiritually on point,

I think that we can be deeply, passionately,

Lustfully Desiring And Connected To Our Wives,

and,at the same time, completely passionate, almost aching to return home to be with our kids instead of trying to avoid parental duties by remaining at the office, hoping they're in bed by the time we get home.

And I believe that in business we can 10x our revenue while covering all of these other areas in our life at the same time, not mutually exclusive."

"Dude, have you been smoking something, bro?" "How the hell are you going to do that?"

"I Don't Know Anybody Who's Pulled All That Shit Off."

I said, "I know. I'm going to be the first one." "Good luck with that."

I leveraged this doubt and the doubt of many others, leaping into what most considered to be a total suicide mission.

Over the next couple of years, I would die and be reborn a hundred times emotionally, leaving behind the old me and awakening to a new version of myself.

In my pursuit to having it all in Body, Being, Balance and Business I came to realize that I was going to need a shitload of training in each area.

Trying to find this kind of training was going to require me to hire coaches, mentors, attend masterminds, read books, articles, newsletters, etc…inside of each one of the four domains of Body, Being, Balance, and Business.

And, if that wasn't enough, I was going to have to learn how to put them all together, gluing the conversation into a comprehensive yet simple system that would allow for a man like myself to actually get, implement, and maintain the game longer than a weekend or even a couple of months.

I Knew Any Asshole Could Do Something Awesome For A Weekend!

(anyone can be a Weekend Warrior)…

…but I was interested in rebuilding my life permanently.

To do this, I needed to change the trajectory of my reality and information, in which guidance and counsel was going to be mandatory.

Although I intellectually understood the price that was having to be paid emotionally, things were 10 times more complicated;

I Had No Fucking Clue How Much Work It Was Really Going To Take.

Just like most parents admit when being honest about having and raising children,

"If I'd known this shit was going to be this hard, I probably wouldn't have had kids."

And yet, you're grateful you did because in that ignorance, you started having babies.

Same goes for pursuing down the paths with Business, and you're like,

"Dude, if I knew it was going to be this hard as an entrepreneur, I don't think I would've done it."

Are You Ready To Pay The Necessary Price?

If I knew how much work, money, literal blood, sweat, and tears it was going to take for me to uncover the Code I call The Warrior's Way to Having It All, I am promising you I would have not taken the journey.

I wouldn't have had the courage, and that is why journeys of a thousand miles begin with just one simple step.

I have spent millions of dollars (yes, you read that right) and tens of thousands of hours, pouring my heart and soul into building and perfecting The Warrior's Way as a predictable System.

It took me four years to discover its use in my life and another Six years proving the concepts of this game with 800+ ELITE high level clients who invested $10k-$250k to train directly with me.

I had to prove that this system could work in the lives of other men, and in order to do that, I needed to develop ten years worth of research and proven data.

The Results in My Own Life

I eventually went from a place in which sex and intimacy in my marriage was only happening once every two to three months to frequently happening two, sometimes three times a week or more.

Not only was it happening, but my wife was actually wanting and desiring me in ways I had never experienced before…and sex was no longer a hunt for a quick vaginal masturbation session.

We have launched our own podcast known as Date Your Wife[7] and co-own multiple business together.

---

7   It has reached the #1 spot inside of iTunes the first few weeks it launched, and continues to remain popular. Go to http://dateyourwifenow.comto watch the latest episodes and read show notes as well as links to our other podcasts inside of the Warrior Empire Network: Date Your Wife co-hosted with my wife Danielle, Big Money Stylist: https:// bigmoneystylisttnow.comwhich is also with Danielle as well as her lead trainers inside of her hair salon, DKW Styling, which specializes in her hair extension technique known as Natural Beaded Rows (NBR), Warrior Wealth: https:// warriorwealthnow.com, Warrior Week: http://warriorweeknow.com,and the Daily Fuel's Warrior On Fire: http:// warrioronfire.com.

My Life In This Area Had Become Un-Fucking-Recognizable To Me From Where I Initially Started.

I went from a disconnected, chaotic relationship with my kids who barely knew their father the banker to wanting and longing to be with my children as much as I could every single day.

I take them to school in the morning and stay up late doing homework with them, ending 90% of my nights lying in bed with each of my babies tickling their backs while we tell stories, pray and listen to meditation music.

My Kids Want To Be Around Dad, And I Want To Be With My Kids.

There is almost never any guilt because I know when and how to choose fatherhood with my children daily so that I gain power from that relationship.

I became the guy who went from complete disconnection as a believer in God to knowing my purpose.

I shifted from following old school religious routines that didn't matter to me while faking my way through to the conversation of Purpose and Divine Power.

In this state of being, I rarely heard the Voice of Revelation and constantly felt as if my life was not on purpose.

Today, I am a man who knows his life is on purpose and when it gets off,

I have tools to help me listen to and trust the Voice inside of me that is guiding me to specific actions.

I have the courage to make decisions that I can't see the end result of, clearly and simply guided by Faith, with a knowing in my heart that when the Voice Speaks it always sees the path clearer than I do.

I went from business destruction, failure and empty bank accounts to rebuilding an Empire in completely different industries while at the same time acquiring Elite Level Skills in Marketing, Selling, Technology, Sequencing,Systems and Leadership.

I Am No Longer A Victim To An Industry Changing Or A Marketplace Shifting.

The Warrior's Way has literally allowed me to guide myself through any dark times in business because the "have it all" lifestyle demands that I see myself as a King equipped with the mindsets and skill sets of Modern Business Mastery.

Truly, For The first Time In My Life,

I Know My Businesses And Bank Accounts Are Under My Control,

and that I am the one determining my destiny.

Within my body, I initially started out as a tired, worn-out shell of a man coming off of three major surgeries, cancer, and 14 months on crutches while shifting several major addictions.

This up and down, year to year roller coaster with my body went from over a decade to a body at almost 42 years of age that is more defined, more shredded, more functional, and more powerful than it was in my early 20s as a high-level elite athlete.

My mindsets and skill-sets in fighting, fitness, endurance, strength, power, performance, consistency and nutrition are at levels that make my life feel bulletproof.

And all this that you just read?

Yeah, it's happening every single day. This is the Life of Kings.

This Is The Life Of Modern Businessmen.

This is the Warrior's Way to Having It All.

Many Warriors have joined Warrior on the brink of divorce, some of them with divorces filed, marriages that are numb, bored, families that are falling apart, businesses that are burning to the ground and watch them not only turn them around but take them to levels that seem to only exist in the movies.

Many of these same men have joined WakeUp Warrior™ with bodies that were jacked up and beaten down from years of addictions, yet have been able to take those shells of abused bodies and turn them into healed weapons of destruction and creation inside their life.

More Fit And On Fire In Their 40's, 50's Than They Ever Were In Their 20's.

Many Warriors have arrived confused about God, their church and beliefs about the system of ideology on the purpose of life, only to level up their understanding with the Divine while experiencing power and purpose at levels they never knew existed.

These men don't sit back like the sedated motherfuckers that we see all over the place who don't take a stand on a damn thing; who allow the media, church leaders, and the schools to teach their children.

They are Kings that have donned the Crown. Warriors who are Waking Up are saying,

"I Am The Creator And The Dictator Of My Life."

Of all the responsibilities in my life that I hold sacred, it is my calling as a Father and Husband that I hold the most dear, the KING inside my own castle to lead my legacy.

If you are able to hear that call as well, why would you return to the shack and live with the peasants and hang out with the whores when you can stand at the top of the Game you've been called to play?

As a king with a queen standing by your side and children who love and adore you?

It is natural to want to place the Crown upon your head and to raise the Title of Liberty in your own life, declaring your desire and intention to Have It All in Body, Being, Balance and Business.

This single declaration will awaken in you a desire to defend and protect the kingdom and to expand the empire in your world with a Fire that will be difficult to control.

The possibility I speak of inside this Brotherhood, inside this conversation, is the Game of Awakening into the life of a Modern Warrior King.

It's Not To Become, But *Awaken* What You Always Were.

Two of the greatest words used in all spiritual writings across all traditions arethese:

"Awaken" And "Remember"

Brother,

Before you and I were even born, the nightmare of Systematic Sedation had begun.

You had no choice with the reality that you were born in the Pit, a hole of male conditioning in which there's nobody to blame and no reason for shame, but you have got to change the game.

And that game starts with you.

So How Do You Change The World, Brother?

You Change One Man...

- If you change a man, you change a marriage.

- If you change a marriage, you change a family.

- If you change a family, you change a community.

- If you change a community, you change a city.

- If you change a city, you change a state.

- If you change a state, you change a country.

- If you change a country, you change the world.

And so it all starts with one man.

Brother, That Man Is You!

Welcome to the revolution of the Wake Up Warrior Movement.

In the hands of a man who is committed to change, this is a very powerful movement.

But not because of me.

Not even because of the tools, strategies, blueprints and systems inside The WarriorBook.

See, WarriorBook and the entire Warrior Movement is like a hammer.

It's Only As Powerful As The Man Swinging It.

Nobody can swing your hammer for you.

Nobody can light a fire in your marriage for you. You must swing your own hammer, Brother.

It starts with The WarriorBook.

If you're ready to go all in with us inside the Brotherhood for you, for your wife, kids and your legacy, we'll gladly welcome you in.

Go grab your copy of the WarriorBook[8] and I'll see you inside.

"Brain-Dead Decisions"

Whether or not to fill up a gas tank on "E" is a pretty "brain-dead decision." Right? If you want to keep driving and going to all the places you want — there's ONLY ONE OPTION.

"Fill that bitch up!" Otherwise, you're going to be stuck.

There's no reason to even think about it. Brother, your life is different. Right now there's an area of your life on "E." Maybe it's your marriage and connection with your children. Maybe it's in your body and you want to weaponize it and feel like an athlete again. Maybe it's in your business and bank account and you want to get off the sidelines and launch your big idea.

You're left with a decision. A "brain-dead decision." You can either breakdown in the middle of the road….Or fill your tank up and follow the map to living the "have-it-all" lifestyle.

---

8   Go to https://warriorbook.comto secure your copy.

ONCE THIS MISSION IS ACCOMPLISHED,
YOUR NEXT STEP IS TO SECURE:

WARRIORBOOK

A MODERN MAN'S GUIDE TO HAVING IT ALL
IN BODY, BEING, BALANCE & BUSINESS

GO TO **WARRIORBOOK.COM**

SECTION FOUR

FUEL FOR YOUR JOURNEY

"I've had confidence in myself all along. It was just a matter getting the pieces back in place."

—Dale Earnhardt, *"The Intimidator"*

[Considered to be one of the best NASCAR drivers of all time, 1951-2001]

"Transformational Gasoline"

(3 Key Principles That Fuel Meaningful Change) Brother,

Creating any meaningful changes in your life is HARD.

I'm Not Going To Bullshit You.

It requires hard fucking work and consistency.

The majority of men who will read this book have found themselves at a place where they were determined to change.

With every fiber of their body and soul they want "MORE" and "BETTER."

- For their wife

- For their children

- For themselves

But not all of them have actually made the changes.

In fact,

Most men don't.

Not because they didn't "want it bad enough."

They Just Ran Out Of Fuel.

I'm sure you've experienced this on some level.

Take "trying to get back in shape" for example.

One day you get fed up enough with how you look and feel and decide to take a stand and do something about it.

You get the gym membership.

You go grocery shopping and buy a bunch of healthy shit.

You might even load up on some supplements, too.

You're Excited And Determined That "This Time It's For Real."

...and in a matter of weeks the motivation has shriveled up and you're already missing workouts and snacking on Cheetos©.

No shame in any of this Brother.

We've all been there.

It's a Fuel game.

You can have the entire trip mapped out, bags packed and car ready to roll.

But without enough fuel to power you through to the desired destination...you'll never get there.

So...

Here's What We Fuel Up On.

I call it Transformational Gasoline...

It consists of 3 simple but powerful principles that keep us focused, inspired and motivated to take massive action and make shit happen.

This is different from The Code, Core 4, The Key 4, The Stack and The General's Tent...

Those are our guiding tools and strategies we use to guide us as we live The Warrior's Way (which you get access to when you buy the Warrior Book[9])

Here's what makes up the Transformational Gasoline:

1- Change Requires Change

Remember what Einstein said...

"A man's mind lacks the capacity to solve the problem it has created at the same level of thinking that originally created the problem."

Meaning…

The man you are today with the mindsets, skillsets, beliefs and perspectives that have ultimately led you into the pit you're stuck in — CANNOT be the same to get you out.

It's IMPOSSIBLE.

This is why you see so many men "TRY really hard" and "WANT really bad" but regardless of what they do, they can never escape their pit.

- It can be seen in the growth or lack thereof in your business.

---

9   To secure your copy for this Manual to living the Warrior's Way, go to: https://warriorbook.com

- It can be seen in all the crucial conversations you've been meaning to have with your wife — but never actually get around to doing it.

- It can be seen in men who don't want to cheat, but keep finding themselves fucking around.

- It can be seen in the man who wants to stop popping pills to wake up, smoking to go to bed and drinking just to be around his family in the evenings…and yet it only continues to get worse.

It's like you're stuck on an island— Hell Island—full of sedation, suppression, disappointment, depression, lies, isolation and stagnation…

…and out in the distance is Heaven Island.

This is where the good shit happens.

- Your connection to your wife and children is over there.

- Your Emotional and Monetary wealth is over there.

- Your strong and athletic body and health is over there.

- Your connection to God and yourself is waiting for you there.

But all you have is a rickety ol' wooden boat that was only good enough to get you as far as Hell Island.

However,it's not nearly big enough, strong enough and stable enough to withstand the current, waves and wind to make it across the water to Heaven Island.

Your "Strong-Will" Can't Magically Make It Come Closer.

Your level of "want" can't calm the waves down.

You can't "positively think" your way over there, either.

The only way off Hell Island and make it to Heaven Island is by turning your boat into a ship.

You need to expand the boat that got you where you are to get where you want to go.

EXPANSION is the name of the game.

It's the only way out of the pit.

How Do You Expand?

That's what the WarriorBook is for.

If you're ready to rapidly grow as a man, father, husband and business man...and you're committed to following the systems, tools and maps we lay out for you in The WarriorBook, Then head on over to https://warriorbook. comand grab a copy for yourself and join our brotherhood.

We'll be waiting for you.

2- Are You Committed?

Listen,

There's been several men "Interested" in transforming their life.

There's been several men "prepared" and "ready to embark on the journey to have-it-all"...

And Yet They Still Die Alone And Miserable.

See,

Transformation and meaningful changes require COMMITMENT, not "interest."

Commitment is pulling the pin on a grenade...

When you pull that motherfucker...you're not going to be "interested" in throwing it —you are fully committed to throwing that bitch.

It's like the raiding Vikings...

When traveling to conquer new territory and expand their kingdom — they would burn their ships on the beach when they landed.

You Think They Were Just "Interested" In Expansion?

They knew they had no choice — there was no "oh well, maybe next time we'll get it…"

They were ALL IN!

Totally. Fucking. Committed.

You might be thinking…

"But Garrett, it's not that serious… I'm not trying to conquer new territories and chuck grenades…I just want to make some more money and be a better husband and father."

While I'll agree with the obvious differences…

I'll Have You Consider,

What's Really At Stake If You Don't Change?

What's going to happen with your marriage?

- Will another man give your wife the love and attention you're not?

- Will you lose your queen to divorce and invite the possibility of another man taking your place as both a husband and a father?

What's going to happen with your kids?

- Is your daughter going to be sleeping with men twice her age because she has validation issues from her lack of connection with you?

- Is your son going to drift and disconnect from you only to turn to drugs and/or alcohol and sedate himself from his lack of feeling worthy because his dad wasn't showing up for him?

Brother,

The reality is this:

You're at a place right now where the action you take or don't take...And the commitment you do or don't have—will shape your legacy and the lives of the people you lead.

- Their sense of self-worth

- Their confidence

- Their courage

- Their growth

- Their entire belief system

All of it is in your hands as their leader to cultivate.

It's A Heavy Burden To Be A KING,

but it's what you signed up for as the man of the house.

I'd say that's a pretty serious place to be...

I'd say those stakes are plenty high to go ALL IN and commit to becoming the man they need you to be.

Wouldn't you?

So...

Let Me Ask You Brother,

- Are you committed to the desires and outcomes you want?

- Are you committed to your wife?

- Are you committed to your children?

- Are you committed to YOU?

- Are you committed to your wealth?

- Are you committed to your health?

I hope so...

If you're not, there's no chance of any meaningful changes to stick in your life.

And if you're NOT committed, The WarriorBook and Brotherhood wouldn't be a good fit for you anyways.

We're All In over here...

If you are too, come join us.

One Day You Will Die.

It can't get more simple than this,

One day you're not going to be here.

That's a fact.

It's the kind of fact most men don't want to dwell on for good reason.

But it's real.

Listen,

You have one shot at this life.

ONE.

- One shot at being a husband to your wife...

- One shot at being a father to your children...

- One shot at creating an impact on this world...

JUST ONE.

The Hard Truth Is This...

One day you or your wife will be going to bed alone.

One day your kids won't be able to call on you to ask for advice, share their wins or just hang out with their dad.

And there may even come an unfathomable day where maybe one of your kids isn't around for you to take out to lunch, pick up from school or play with in the backyard.

THAT SHIT IS REAL.

This isn't some bullshit "emotional tactic."

It's real, fucking life.

- Men die.

- Women die.

- Children die.

It's a painful reality, but the sooner you truly realize how precious and fragile life is,the sooner you'll get off the fucking sidelines and jump in the game as the LEADER you are...

...Instead of acting like there's always going to be time to "make up for it."

When You Fully Grasp This Principle...

- *It becomes easier* to wake up earlier in the morning to have more time in the evenings with your family.

- *It becomes easier* to turn your phone off and just be present with your family.

- *It becomes easier* to treat your wife with the respect, love, appreciation and gratitude that she deserves.

- *It becomes easier* to show up for your kids as a father who is committed, vulnerable, emotionally available, fun and a leader.

- *It becomes easie*r to actively invest in yourself and take aggressive action to expand your business and bank accounts.

Brother, I get it if you're reading this, feeling like I'm raining down guilt bombs on you.

As if I'm just trying to make you feel bad about yourself.

I've been there before and so have thousands of other brothers who have come through Warrior.

Believe Me, You're NOT Alone!

My goal here isn't to "make you feel guilty."

My goal is to make you wake up to the truth and reality.

I don't have a say in the specific emotions that get evoked inside of you as a result.

It's going to be different for everyman.

The KEY is to allow those emotions to pour over you. Don't avoid it, embrace it…and USE it as fuel to do something about it.

"Feelings" May Be Painful And Uncomfortable,

but they're short-lived and they lead you to the truth, guiding you towards taking action.

We use the system known as "The Stack" to leverage our feelings and emotions to help us see the truth and to make key decisions.

If you've ever wondered how Warrior grew as big and as fast as it did over such a short period of time…it's in large part due to The Stack.

Most of the men in the Brotherhood are seeing more results in 90 days than they did in the last 24 months thanks to The Stack.

It's an absolutely vital tool that we use EVERY. SINGLE. DAY. as part of our **Core4.**

I teach the entire "Stack System" as well as the "Core 4" routine in the WarriorBook[10].

THE ROCKET FUEL...

If there was ever a "secret sauce" to what makes WarriorBook so powerful and effective…

It would be the fact that WE DON'T PLAY THIS GAME ALONE.

When you buy the WarriorBook, you get access to a brotherhood of men who live by the same code, use the same tools, the same systems and same processes together as a unit…collectively supporting and holding one another accountable.

There's a sense of peace, excitement, hope and certainty that comes with being on a team full of men who completely understand you and share many of the exact same desires and struggles you do.

Inside of this place where you're "not feeling alone," you get access to the space you need to stop lying and begin showing up as ALL of you.

---

10   To gain access to the power of The Stack today, go to https://warriorbook.com

You Can Take The Mask Off.

You can ask questions and get answers.

You can get clarity.

Once this begins to happen, you can start extracting power and productivity you never imagined you had that opens up a whole new world of opportunities and possibilities with your business, marriage, children and health.

The body you never thought you'd ever get back — you will.

The Marriage You Thought Was Doomed — Will Be Reignited.

The business that was stalled out, robbing you of energy — will finally give you the freedom and wealth you once thought was just a pipe dream.

All of which has been made possible from fueling up on transformational gasoline, joining a powerful group of men to support you and leveraging the tools, systems and strategies inside the WarriorBook.

This game is not meant to be played alone.

Remember,

Lies, Sedation And Suppression Feed Off Of Isolation.

With programs like The WarriorBook, you now know isolation is a choice you don't have to make if you don't want to.

You simply don't have to feel alone anymore.

There's a way out.

There's a community of men living by a Code, willing to help you use the tools, tactics and strategies from The WarriorBook to help you get out of your Pit.

All you have to do is choose expansion, liberation and a brotherhood over lies, sedation, suppression and isolation.

It's up to you.

Two Things I Know About You

The fact that you're reading this book tells me two things about you.

1. You know there's more to life than what you're currently experiencing for both yourself and your family.

2. You obviously love yourself and your family enough to take the first step towards fixing it, by checking this whole "warrior thing"out.

Both of these put you ahead of where most men are at. But what I still don't know about you is this…Are you committed to yourself and your family enough to take THE NEXT STEP?

Are you ready to jump in this game with me and the rest of the men inside of the Brotherhood to start living the 4 Dimensional Life of Having It All?

They deserve it, and so do you, Brother.

ONCE THIS MISSION IS ACCOMPLISHED,
YOUR NEXT STEP IS TO SECURE:

WARRIORBOOK

A MODERN MAN'S GUIDE TO HAVING IT ALL
IN BODY, BEING, BALANCE & BUSINESS

GO TO WARRIORBOOK.COM

SECTION FIVE

"TIME'S UP"

"Unfortunately, the clock is ticking, the hours are going by. The past increases, the future recedes. Possibilities decreasing, regrets mounting."

—Haruki Murakami
[Contemporary Japanese Writer and Translator, 1949-]

Whatever You Do, Don't Get Stuck Here...

What Does This Picture...

...Have to do with the amount of money you make, the amount of sex you have and the relationship you have with your wife and kids?

I'll share the answer with you in a minute.

For most men,

The picture you just saw represents why most men can't get out of their own way and stay stuck in their bullshit.

Remember...

Your Life,

Where it is today...

Is A Result Of The Action and Inaction You Have Taken.

- Your body is a reflection of the action and inaction you have taken.

- Your spiritual connection is a reflection of the action and inaction you have taken.

- Your marriage and family life is a reflection of the action and inaction you have taken.

- Your business is a reflection of the action and inaction you have taken.

Again,

Easy enough concept to grasp and agree with...

Correct?

So, Answer this question:

What's Going To Change?

If you're reading this book — you know there's more for you.

You know you're playing small and not showing up as the leader you need to be to your family and in your business.

You know you could be making more money.

You know your marriage needs a fire lit under it.

You know how important it is for you to show up as the father and leader your children need and count on.

What's going to change?

We've already established the laws of nature proclaim you must become more to get more.

As you come to the conclusion of this book...

...And the final page gets turned,

WHAT ARE YOU GOING TO DO, TO EXPAND THE MAN YOU ARE TODAY, TO GET THE RESULTS YOU DESIRE IN YOUR BODY, FAMILY, SPIRITUALITY, BUSINESS AND BANK ACCOUNT, TOMORROW?

Here's What I Know.

Unless you have already bought the WarriorBook, or you've already decided to tell me to "fuck-off."

(Both of which I'm cool with)

The reality is this...

You're currently sitting in a place that destroys most men.

A place that keeps you playing small…constantly second guessing…losing focus…stressed… overwhelmed… afraid that life and time is getting away from you… confused…wanting more and trying harder but never getting the result…

This place is called THE FENCE.

The fence is that thing you "sit on" when you're facing a big or small opportunity or challenge.

(They're often the same thing)

The Fence is what holds you back from decisive action when you have a big chance staring you right in your eyes.

The Fence is what keeps you inside your comfort zone and afraid of changing things up even though intellectually you understand it's a must to get what you want.

Right Now You Might Be Sitting Squarely On The Fence With The WarriorBook.

And Brother, I get it.

I've wasted years on the fence with a lot of shit.

But I want you to understand something.

The "fence" you're sitting on has NOTHING to do with me or WarriorBook.

It's Much Bigger Than That.

Of course, I'd love to chat and interact with you in the Brotherhood after you invest in the WarriorBook.

But here's the thing…

If you don't want it,

That's ok.

Just commit to saying "no" right now and don't buy the book.

I don't need to rely on corny sales tactics to get men to invest in the Warrior Book.

This is REAL SHIT.

There are "fences" in your life every day, all around you, and you constantly sit on them in a constant state of "about to…" and "I was meaning to…"

Here's How Most Fences Show Up In A Man's Life.

—> You want to hire a personal trainer and nutritionist to finally get in shape…but you never actually do it….and you also never actually say you're not going to either.

Instead, you just sit perched up on the fence.

So deep in the bullshit you can't commit to yes or no.

—> It shows up as a business man who claims he's going to launch this product, write that book, build a new funnel…

But years later, it's still in the "idea stage" being mentally masturbated on.

Why Don't You Just Say You're NOT Going To Do It?

(I'll tell you why in a minute)

—> **How many times** have you been on the fence about having a routine to shut your phone off and being present with your family in the evenings… but never doit?

—> **How many times** were you going to have "that conversation" with your wife?

—> **How many times** did you know you needed to apologize to your wife, son or daughter but didn't doit?

—> **How many times** have you told yourself you're going to do date nights? …reach out to a friend…spend more time with your children?

Only to never do it, then lie to yourself that "next time" you'll make it happen?

Once You Start Living This Way It Becomes Very Dangerous For A Man.

The thing about "I'll start next Monday" or "I'll do it next time" is in actuality code for "probably NEVER."

And by holding on to the belief that "one day I'll get around to it" (even though you're not) — it's a way to get yourself off the hook from ever having to doit.

It's a way to sedate from feeling the pressure and accountability of actually doing something outside of your comfort zone.

It's a way to hide from the judgment that might come your way for taking a stand and making a commitment.

Residing In The Land Of Yes And No

Results and expansion happen in the land of"yes" and"no."

"Maybe" is the fence that divides the two lands where NOTHING can grow.

And the results from living a life on the fence has you…

Disconnected From Your Family

- Out-of-shape and unhealthy

- Stressed, stagnant and overwhelmed in your business or career

- Talking a big game but playing a small one

- Always knowing what to do, but never doing it.

Brother,

The time to get off the fence is NOW.

And it begins with the WarriorBook.

"BE THE MAN" is about discovering WHERE you are and WHY you must shift to start living as a four-dimensional man

The WarriorBook is all about how to pull it off.

People ask me all of the time,

"How is it you can claim to have a science and system for a lifestyle?"

"How can you make such big and bold claims about men having more sex and making more money from reading a *book*?"

There's two reasons:

1-It's Not Just A Book.

It's an interactive experience.

Yes, there's a book you get (and it's a powerful one) but you also get access to software, email sequences and video trainings to go along with the book.

More importantly you get access to a Brotherhood full of men who LIVE by the same Code, who are WILLING and READY to support you and hold you accountable to becoming the man, entrepreneur, father and husband you want to be.

2-We Have A Process.

As you'll soon see when you get the WarriorBook,

There's an entire system for living the have it all lifestyle, complete with…

- **A Code we live by** and stand on that guides us in everything we do.

- **Daily Actions and routines** we call The Core 4 that reduces stress, creates clarity and guarantees expansion across all 4 areas of your life—Body, Being (Spirituality), Balance (Family), and Business—if you follow it consistently.

- **Weekly Actions for increased productivity** and expansion specifically inside our businesses and/

or careers we call Key 4…Plus a weekly review to optimize the process and pace for the upcoming week we call The General's Tent.

- **Quarterly Actions** set up by our 90-Day Challenges which are engineered in a unique way to accelerate results across all 4 areas of your life.

We do all this by leveraging Tactical Blueprints, Tools, Doctrine, Sequences and Maps that allow Men to Achieve Predictable and Repeatable Results Time and Time again.

I Want To Invite You To Get Off The Fence...

…and join the thousands of committed men who took action, Invested In the book and transformed their lives using the "have-it-all" system and tools that you'll get access to immediately after you Invest In the WarriorBook.

But you must decide: yes or no. No more maybes…no more fences.

It's been keeping you stuck long enough.

Either say "fuck no" and put this paperback on the shelf to collect dust.

Or say "fuck yes" and head over to https:// warriorbook. com and buy it now (if there are any copies left).

But no maybes….no "I'll do it later."

Remember…

At This point, Isolation Is A Choice.

You don't have to play this game alone, There's a group of men, including me, who are waiting on you to join us, who are beyond willing to welcome you into the Brotherhood and support you on your journey to having it all.

We're here for you, Brother.

Will you join us?

The choice is yours…Choose Wisely.

With HONOR and RESPECT.

The End. Garrett J White

ABOUT THE AUTHOR

Garrett J White is the founder of Wake Up Warrior™ and creator of the WarriorBook. Garrett's revolutionary training program has influenced men around the world and can be heard on a regular basis with his top-rated podcasts across multiple platforms from family & parenting with his wife, Danielle, on *Date Your Wife* to Business with *Warrior Wealth* and *Big Money Stylist* (which is also top rated in the hair industry), Religion & Spirituality with *Warrior On Fire* and Self Development with *Warrior Week.* Garrett lives in Laguna Beach,California where he surfs everyday.